EASY GUITAR WITH NOTES & TAB

THE BEST OF Ozzy Osbourne
14 SONGS PLUS GUITAR SOLOS

Cover photo: Ross Halfin

ISBN 978-0-634-01367-6

Hal•Leonard CORPORATION

7777 W. BLUEMOUND RD. P.O. BOX 13819 MILWAUKEE, WI 53213

Visit Hal Leonard Online at
www.halleonard.com

Guitar Notation Legend

Guitar Music can be notated three different ways: on a *musical staff*, in *tablature*, and in *rhythm slashes*.

RHYTHM SLASHES are written above the staff. Strum chords in the rhythm indicated. Use the chord diagrams found at the top of the first page of the transcription for the appropriate chord voicings. Round noteheads indicate single notes.

THE MUSICAL STAFF shows pitches and rhythms and is divided by bar lines into measures. Pitches are named after the first seven letters of the alphabet.

TABLATURE graphically represents the guitar fingerboard. Each horizontal line represents a string, and each number represents a fret.

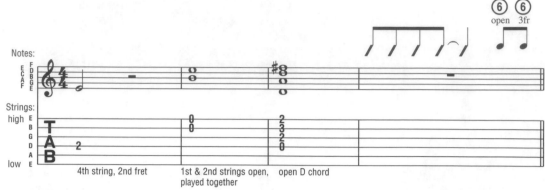

HALF-STEP BEND: Strike the note and bend up 1/2 step.

WHOLE-STEP BEND: Strike the note and bend up one step.

GRACE NOTE BEND: Strike the note and immediately bend up as indicated.

SLIGHT (MICROTONE) BEND: Strike the note and bend up 1/4 step.

BEND AND RELEASE: Strike the note and bend up as indicated, then release back to the original note. Only the first note is struck.

PRE-BEND: Bend the note as indicated, then strike it.

VIBRATO: The string is vibrated by rapidly bending and releasing the note with the fretting hand.

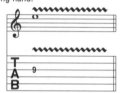

WIDE VIBRATO: The pitch is varied to a greater degree by vibrating with the fretting hand.

HAMMER-ON: Strike the first (lower) note with one finger, then sound the higher note (on the same string) with another finger by fretting it without picking.

PULL-OFF: Place both fingers on the notes to be sounded. Strike the first note and without picking, pull the finger off to sound the second (lower) note.

LEGATO SLIDE: Strike the first note and then slide the same fret-hand finger up or down to the second note. The second note is not struck.

SHIFT SLIDE: Same as legato slide, except the second note is struck.

TRILL: Very rapidly alternate between the notes indicated by continuously hammering on and pulling off.

TAPPING: Hammer ("tap") the fret indicated with the pick-hand index or middle finger and pull off to the note fretted by the fret hand.

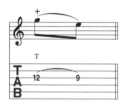

NATURAL HARMONIC: Strike the note while the fret-hand lightly touches the string directly over the fret indicated.

PINCH HARMONIC: The note is fretted normally and a harmonic is produced by adding the edge of the thumb or the tip of the index finger of the pick hand to the normal pick attack.

PICK SCRAPE: The edge of the pick is rubbed down (or up) the string, producing a scratchy sound.

MUFFLED STRINGS: A percussive sound is produced by laying the fret hand across the string(s) without depressing, and striking them with the pick hand.

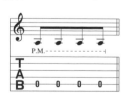

PALM MUTING: The note is partially muted by the pick hand lightly touching the string(s) just before the bridge.

RAKE: Drag the pick across the strings indicated with a single motion.

TREMOLO PICKING: The note is picked as rapidly and continuously as possible.

VIBRATO BAR DIVE AND RETURN: The pitch of the note or chord is dropped a specified number of steps (in rhythm) then returned to the original pitch.

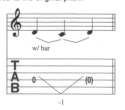

VIBRATO BAR SCOOP: Depress the bar just before striking the note, then quickly release the bar.

VIBRATO BAR DIP: Strike the note and then immediately drop a specified number of steps, then release back to the original pitch.

STRUM AND PICK PATTERNS

This chart contains the suggested strum and pick patterns that are referred to by number at the beginning of each song in this book. The symbols ⊓ and ∨ in the strum patterns refer to down and up strokes, respectively. The letters in the pick patterns indicate which right-hand fingers plays which strings.

p = **thumb**
i = **index finger**
m = **middle finger**
a = **ring finger**

For example; Pick Pattern 2
is played: thumb - index - middle - ring

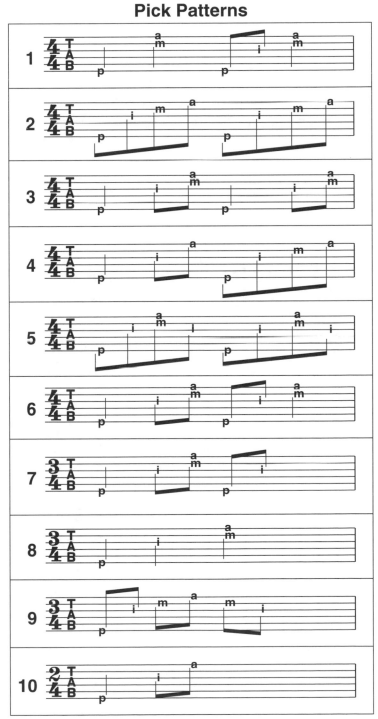

You can use the 3/4 Strum or Pick Patterns in songs written in compound meter (6/8, 9/8, 12/8, etc.).
For example, you can accompany a song in 6/8 by playing the 3/4 pattern twice in each measure.
The 4/4 Strum and Pick Patterns can be used for songs written in cut time (¢) by doubling the note time values in the patterns. Each pattern would therefore last two measures in cut time.

Bark at the Moon

Words and Music by Ozzy Osbourne

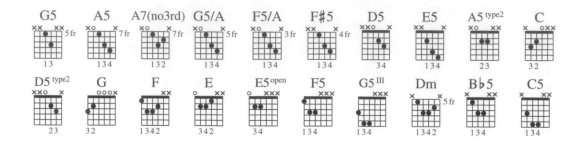

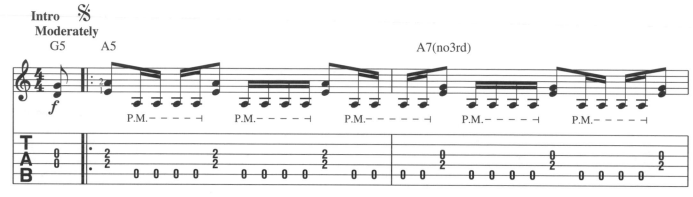

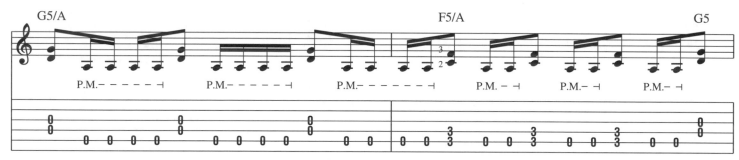

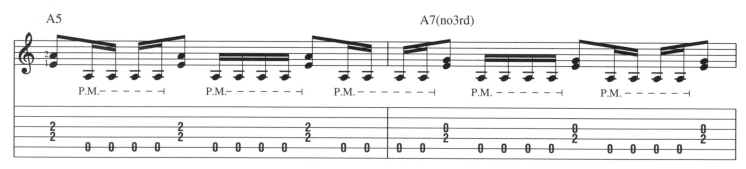

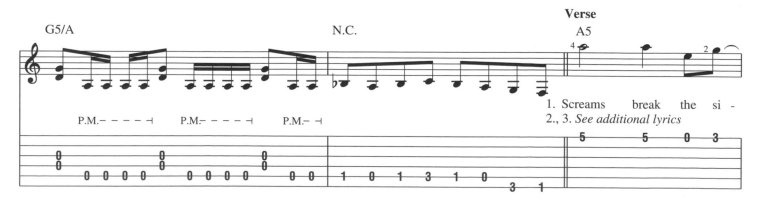

1. Screams break the si -
2., 3. *See additional lyrics*

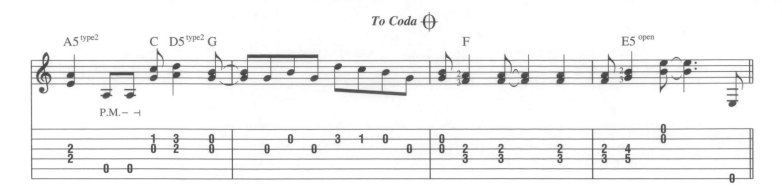

Bridge
Half-time feel

They cursed and bur-ied him a-long with _____ shame _

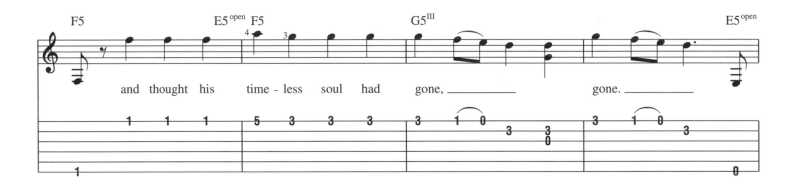

and thought his time-less soul had gone, _____ gone. _____

In emp-ty burn-ing hell, un-ho-ly _____ one, _

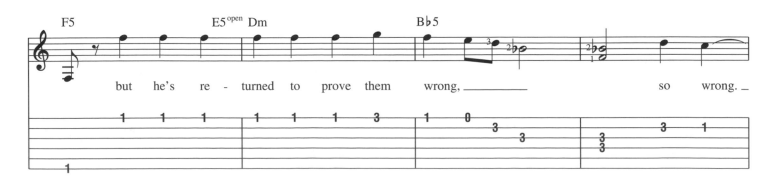

but he's re-turned to prove them wrong, _____ so wrong. _

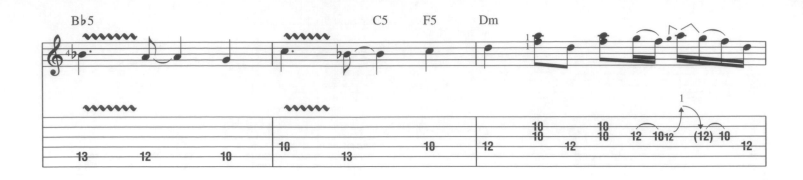

D.S. al Coda

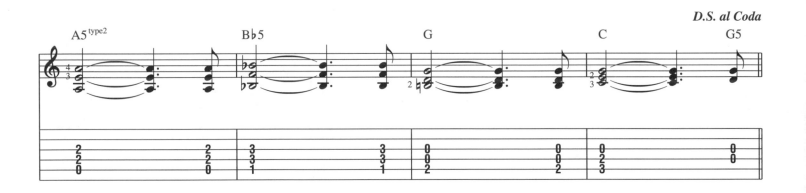

⊕ **Coda**

Hey, _____ yeah, bark at the moon.

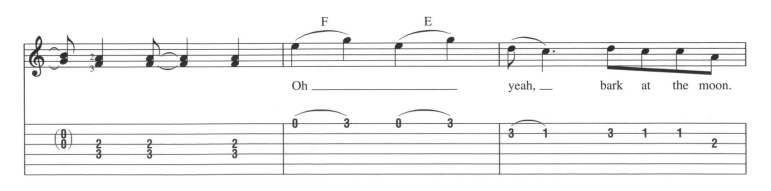

Oh _____ yeah, __ bark at the moon.

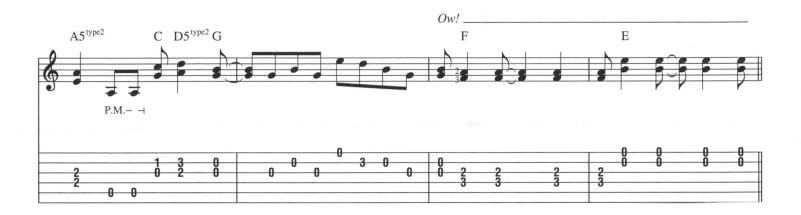

Outro

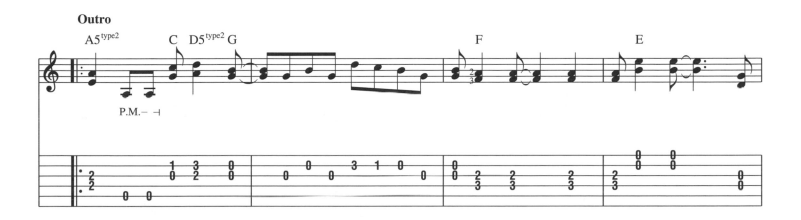

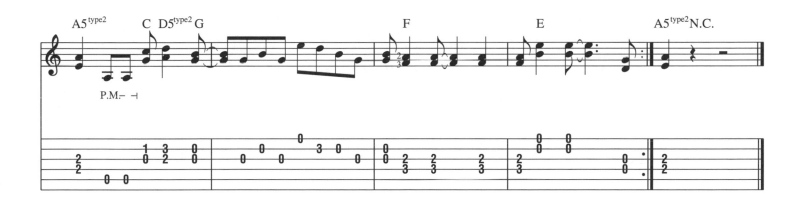

Additional Lyrics

2. Years spent in torment,
   Buried in a nameless grave.
   Now he has risen.
   Miracles would have to save.

Pre-Chorus 2., 3. Those that the beast is looking for,
   Listen in awe and you'll hear him
   Bark at the moon.

3. Howling in shadows,
   Living in a lunar spell.
   He finds his heaven
   Spewing from the mouth of hell.

Crazy Train

Words and Music by Ozzy Osbourne, Randy Rhoads and Bob Daisley

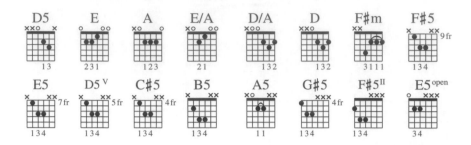

Strum Pattern: 2
Pick Pattern: 4

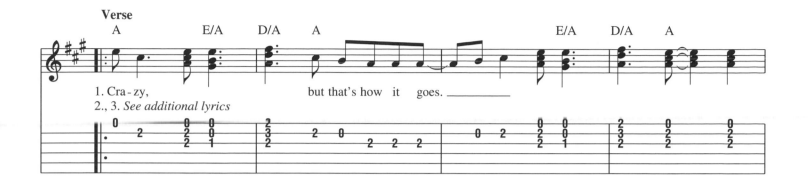

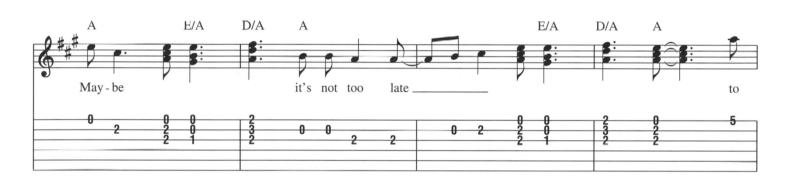

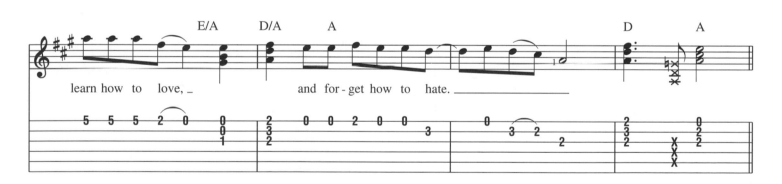

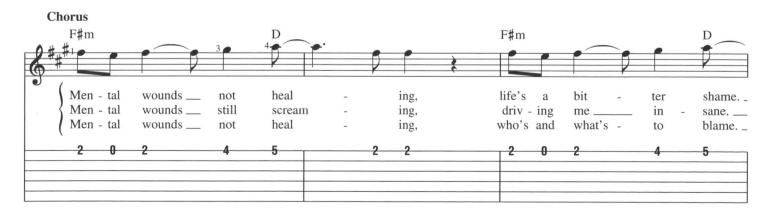

I'm go-ing off ___ the rails ___ on a cra-zy train. ___

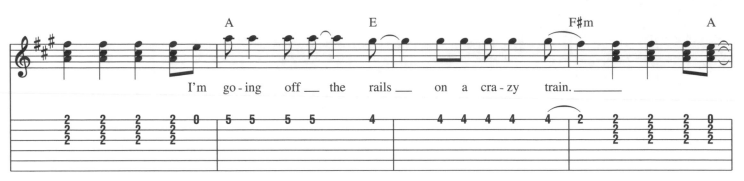

I'm go-ing off ___ the rails ___ on a cra-zy train. _____

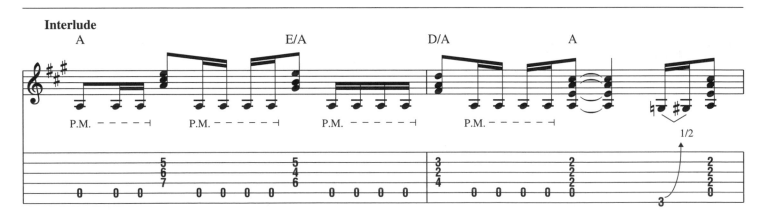

To Coda ⊕

Spoken: Let's go!

Interlude

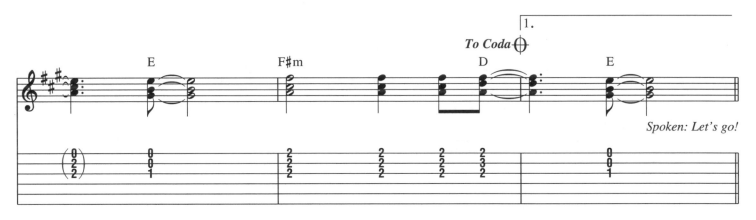

2. I've

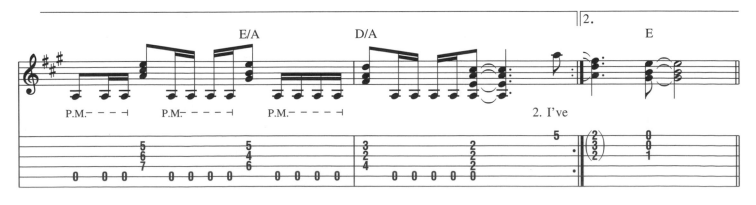

Bridge

I know that __ things _ are _ go - ing wrong for me. __

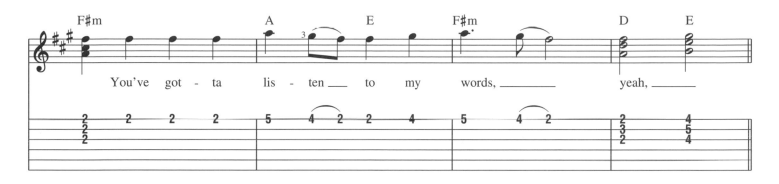

You've got - ta lis - ten __ to my words, _____ yeah, _____

Guitar Solo

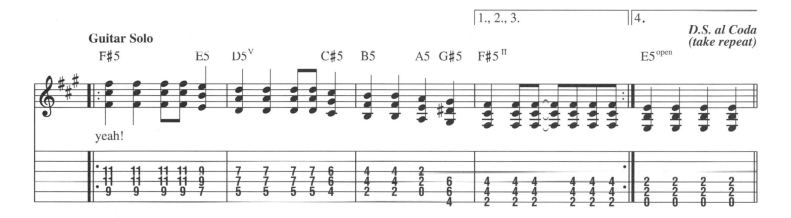

yeah!

D.S. al Coda
(take repeat)

⊕ **Coda**

Outro

Repeat and fade

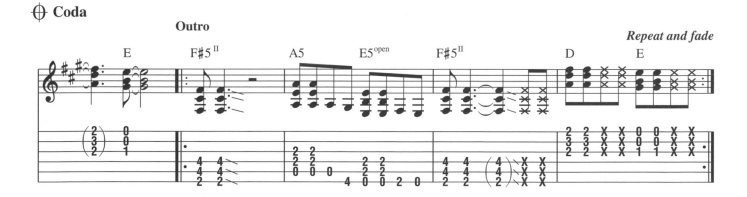

Additional Lyrics

2. I've listened to preachers, I've listened to fools.
   I've watched all the dropouts who make their own rules.
   One person conditioned to rule and control.
   The media sells it, and you live the role.

3. Heirs of a cold war, that's what we've become.
   Inheriting troubles, I'm mentally numb.
   Crazy, I just cannot bear.
   I'm living with something that just isn't fair.

Dee

Music by Randy Rhoads

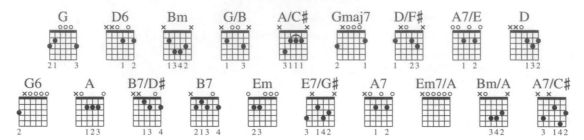

Strum Pattern: 8
Pick Pattern: 8

Moderately fast

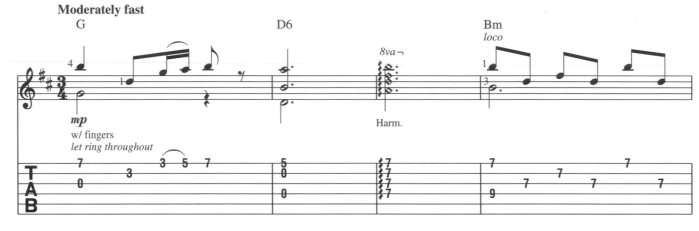

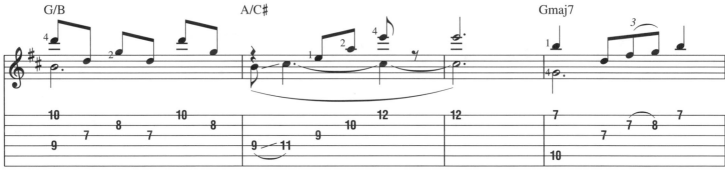

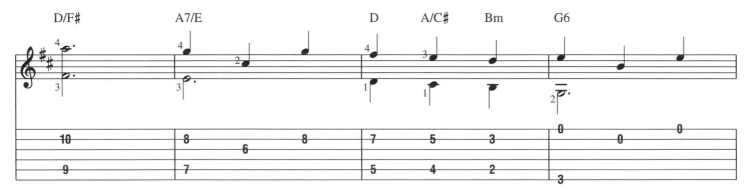

Flying High Again

Words and Music by Ozzy Osbourne, Randy Rhoads, Bob Daisley and Lee Kerslake

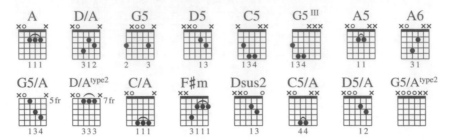

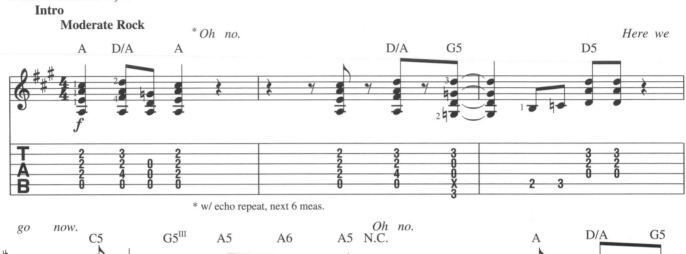

Strum Pattern: 2, 4
Pick Pattern: 2, 4

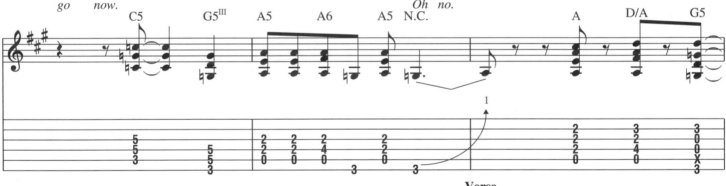

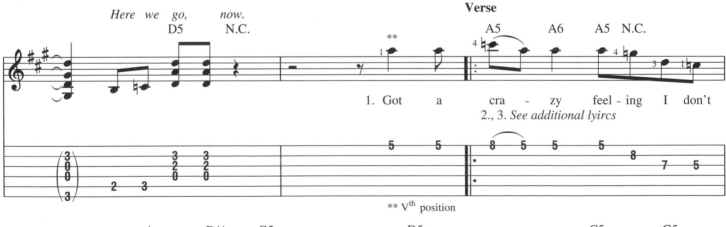

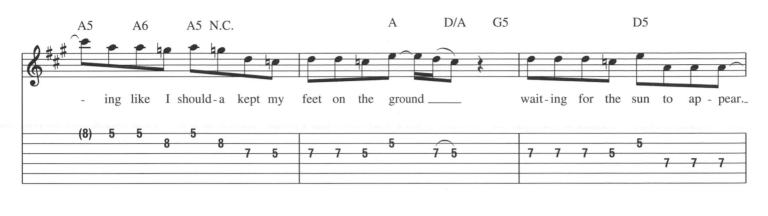

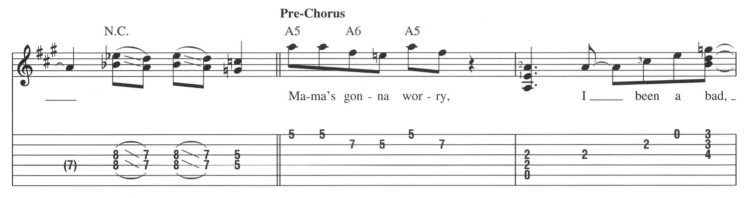

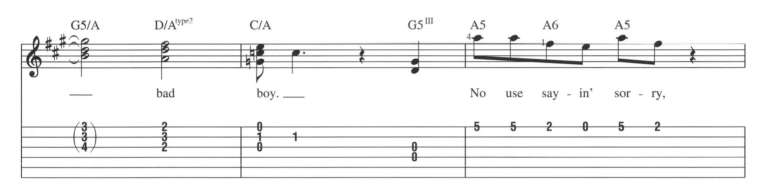

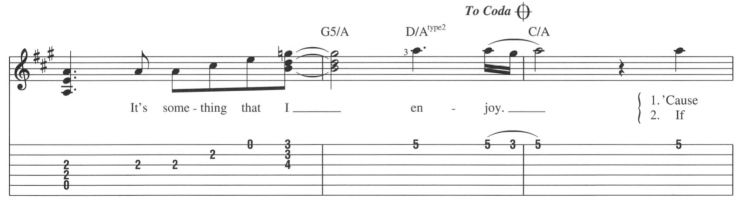

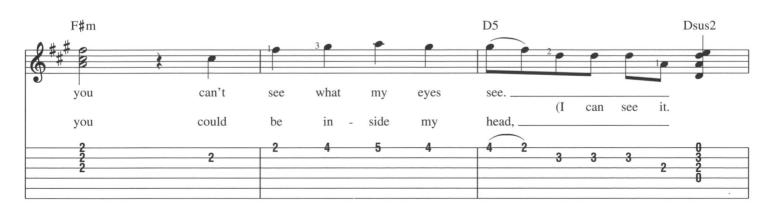

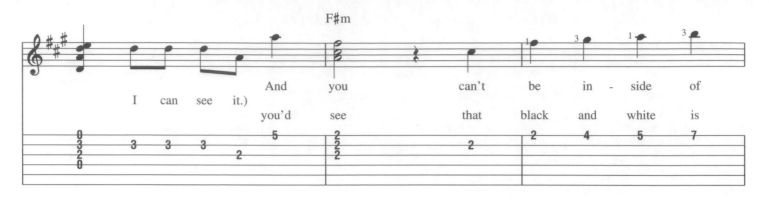

And you can't be in - side of

I can see it.) you'd see that black and white is

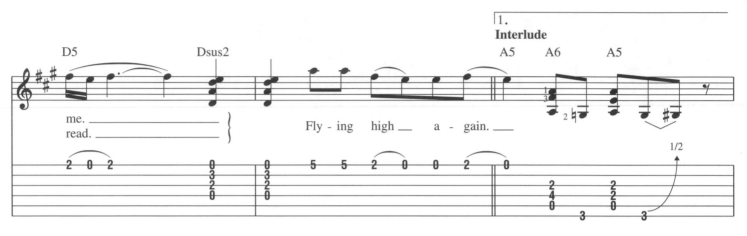

me. Fly - ing high a - gain.
read.

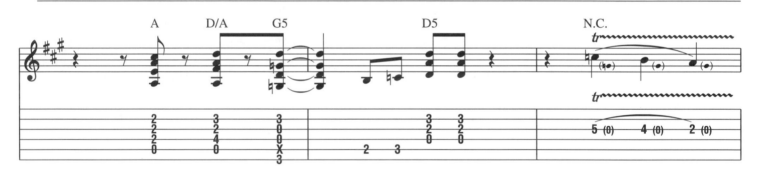

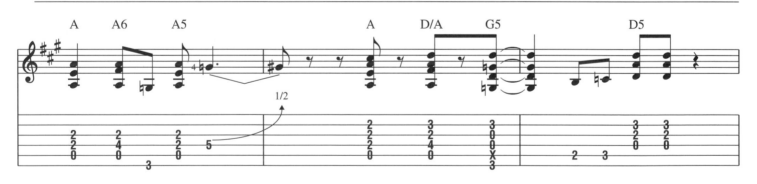

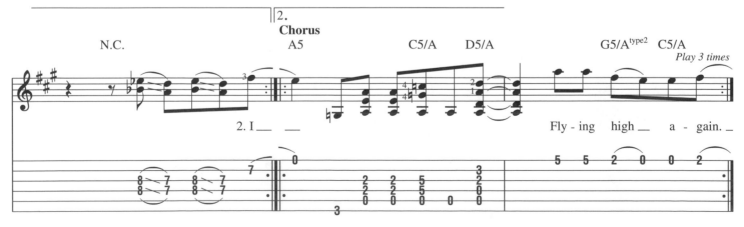

2. I Fly - ing high a - gain.

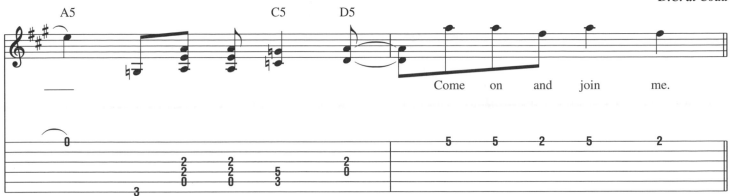

Come on and join me.

Coda

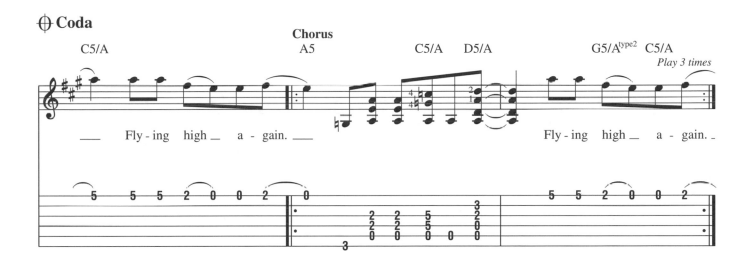

Chorus

___ Fly - ing high ___ a - gain. ___

Play 3 times

Fly - ing high ___ a - gain. ___

Outro

Repeat and fade

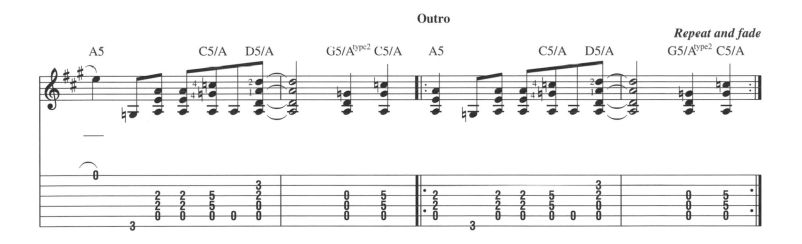

Additional Lyrics

2. I can see through mountains, watch me disappear.
   I can even touch the sky.
   Swallowing colors of the sound I hear.
   Am I just a crazy guy? You bet.

3. Daddy thinks I'm lazy, he don't understand,
   Never saw inside my head.
   People think I'm crazy, but I'm in demand,
   Never heard a thing I said.

Goodbye to Romance

Words and Music by John Osbourne, Robert Daisley and Randy Rhoads

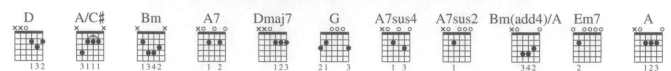

D   A/C#   Bm   A7   Dmaj7   G   A7sus4   A7sus2   Bm(add4)/A   Em7   A

Strum Pattern: 5
Pick Pattern: 3

Intro
Slowly

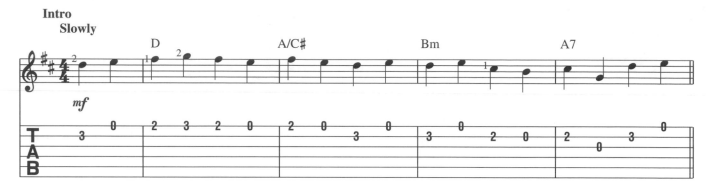

Verse

1. Yes - ter - day __ has been and gone. __ To - mor - row, will __ I find the sun __ or
2. *See additional lyrics*

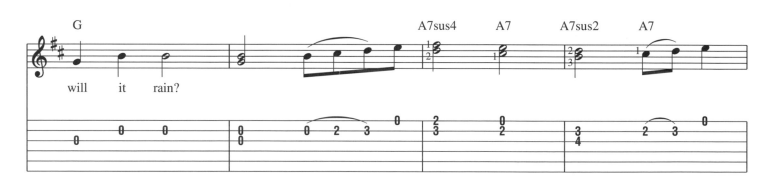

will it rain?

Dmaj7

Ev - 'ry - bod - y's hav - ing fun __ ex - cept me, I'm __ the lone - ly one, __ I

live in shame. I said,

%℄ Chorus

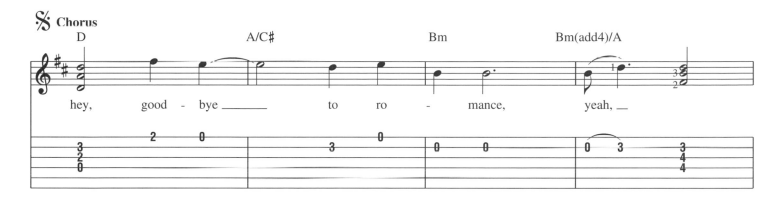

hey, good - bye to ro - mance, yeah, __

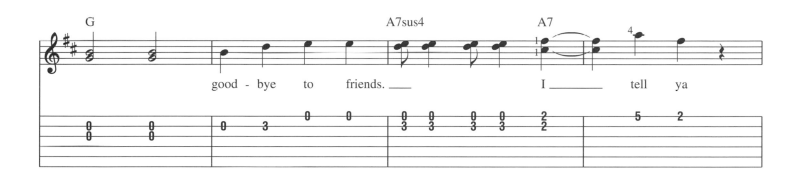

good - bye to friends. __ I __ tell ya

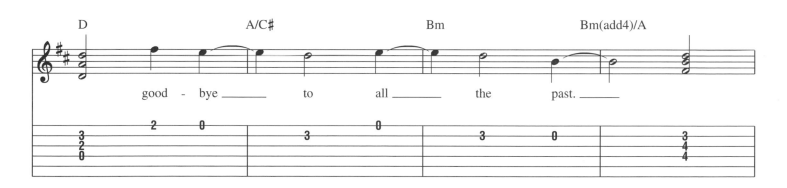

good - bye __ to all __ the past. __

To Coda 1 ⊕
To Coda 2 ⊕

I guess that we'll meet, __ we'll meet in the end. __

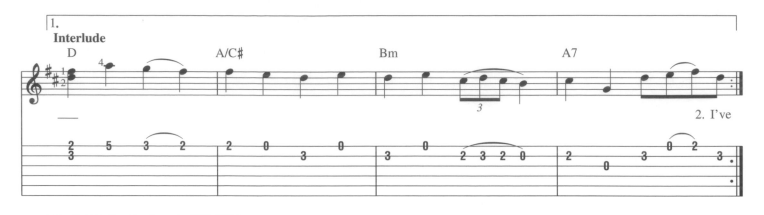

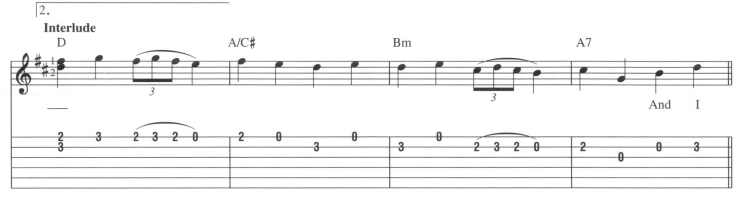

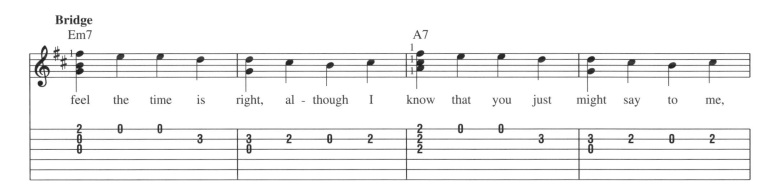

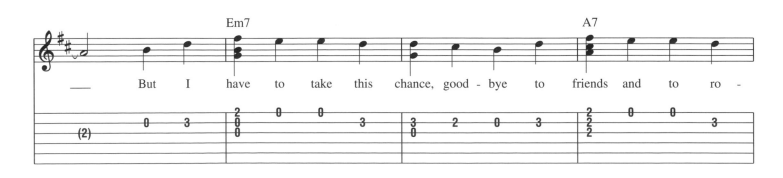

mance _____ and to all ___ of you, _____

Guitar Solo

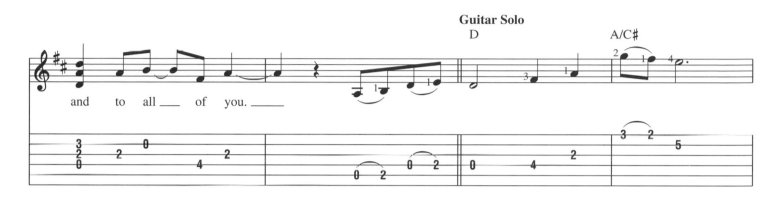

and to all ___ of you. _____

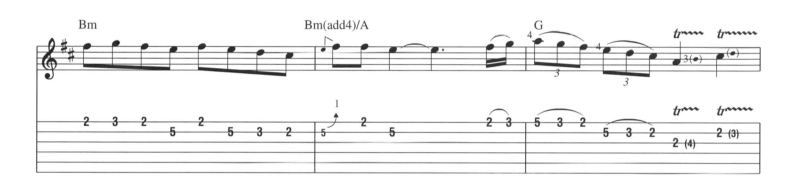

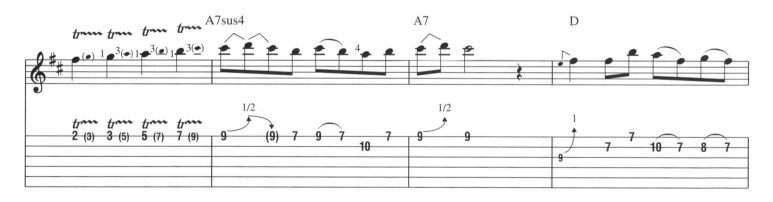

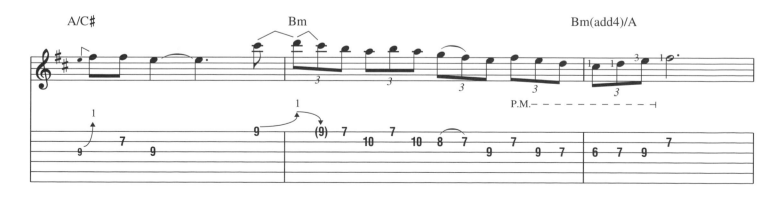

⊕ Coda 1

Interlude

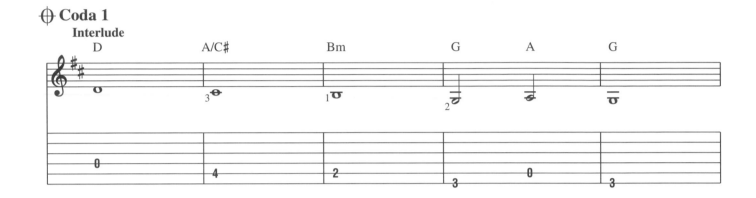

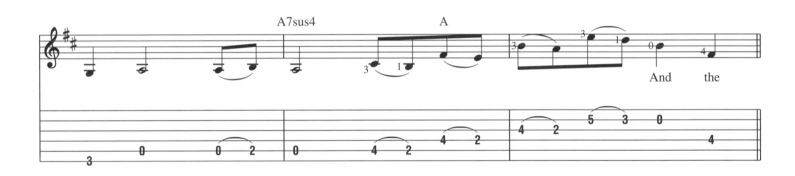

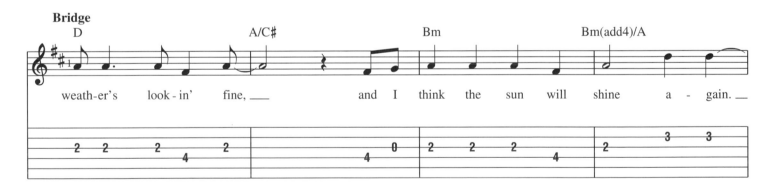

Bridge

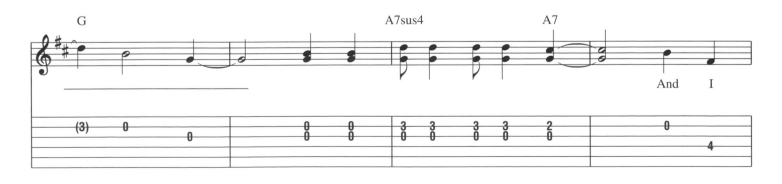

feel   I've cleared my   mind,   all   the   past   is   left   be - hind   a - gain. __

D.S. al Coda 2

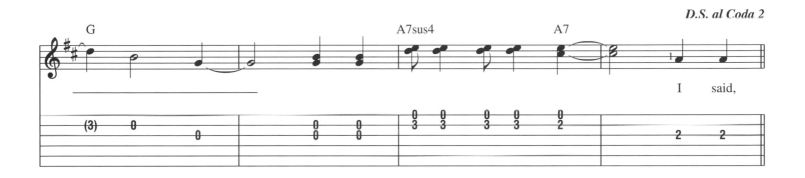

I   said,

⊕ Coda 2
Outro

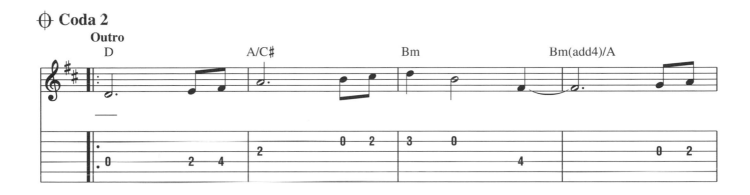

Repeat and fade

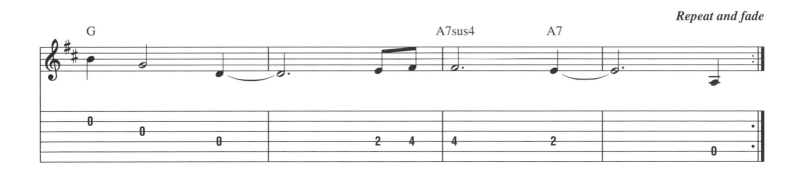

Additional Lyrics

2. I've been the king, I've been the clown.
   Now broken wings can't hold me down,
   I'm free again.
   The jester with the broken crown,
   It won't be me this time around
   To love in vain.

I Don't Know

Words and Music by Ozzy Osbourne, Randy Rhoads and Bob Daisley

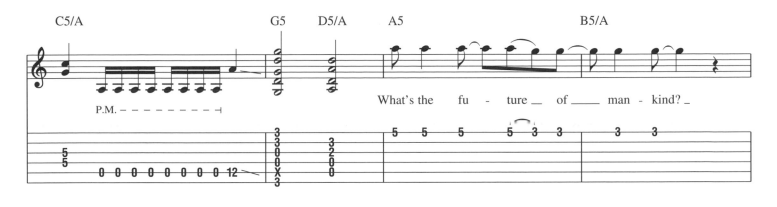

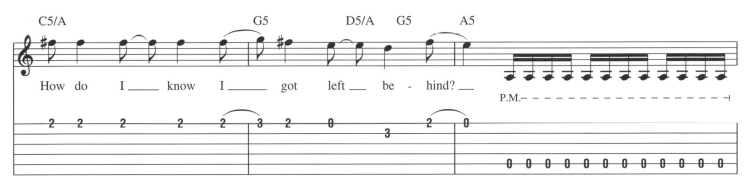

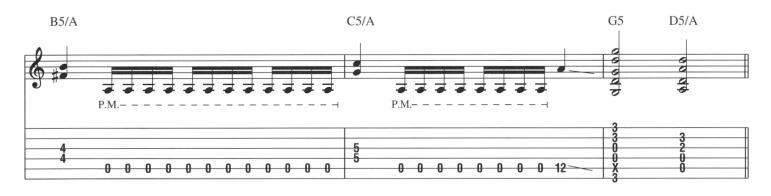

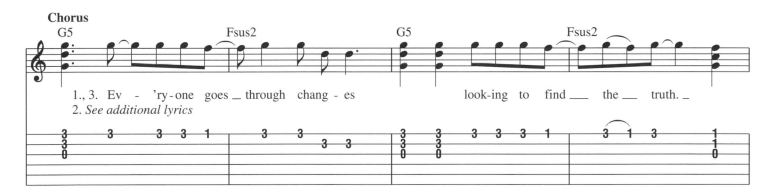

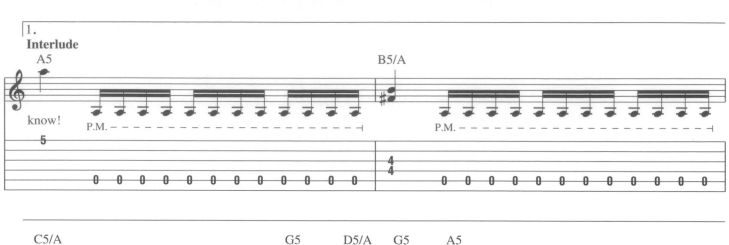

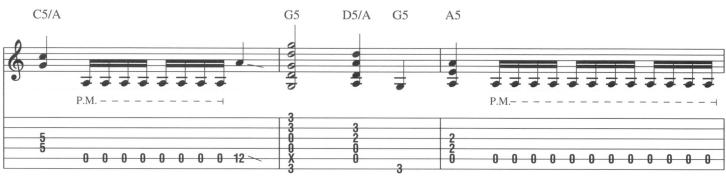

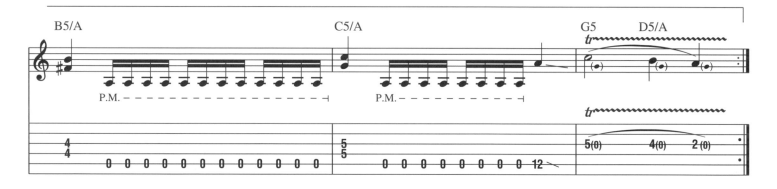

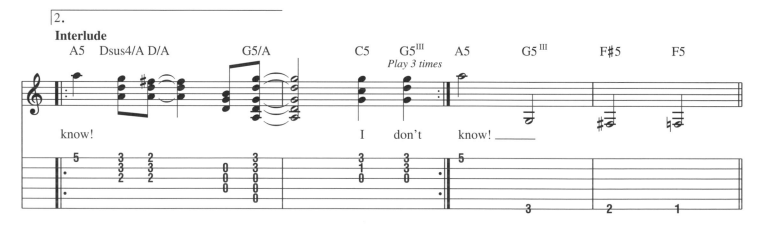

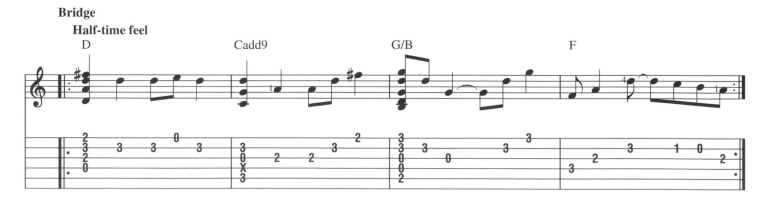

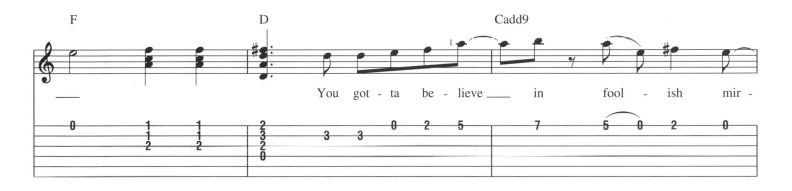

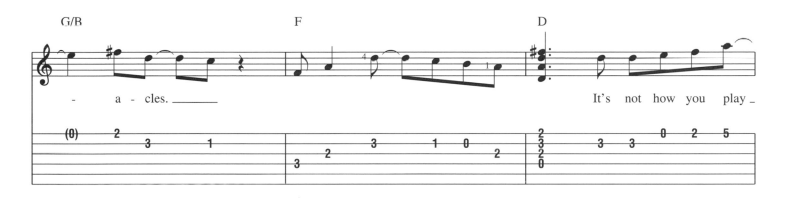

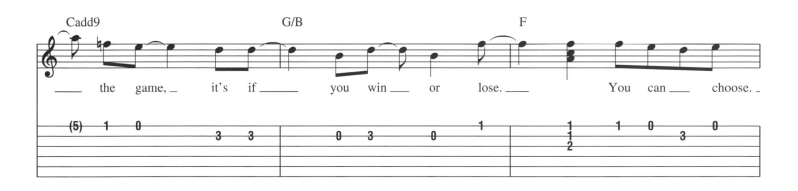

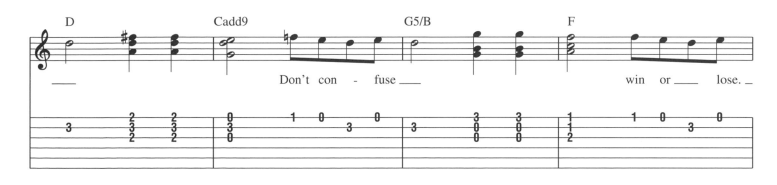

Additional Lyrics

2. How am I supposed to know
   Hidden meanings that will never show?
   Fools and prophets from the past,
   Life's a stage and we're all in the cast.

Chorus 2. You gotta believe in someone,
   Asking me who is right.
   Asking me who to follow.
   Don't ask me, I don't know!

Mama, I'm Coming Home

Words and Music by Ozzy Osbourne and Zakk Wylde

Strum Pattern: 1
Pick Pattern: 2

Intro

Moderately slow

mp
w/ pick & fingers
let ring throughout

Verse

1. Times have changed, __ and times are strange. __ Here I come, __ but I ain't the same. ___

Ma - ma, I'm com - ing home. __

Times gone by, ___ it seems to be, ___ you could've been _ a bet - ter friend to me. ___

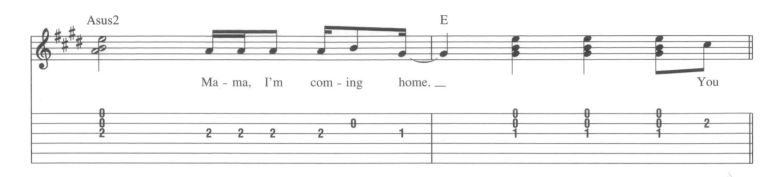

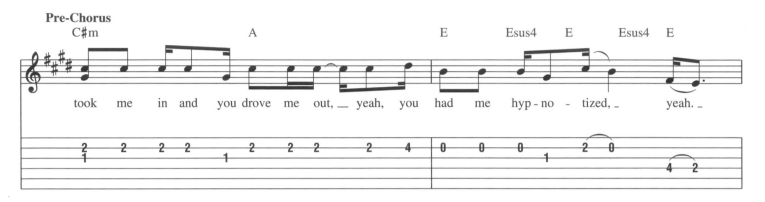

Pre-Chorus

Verse

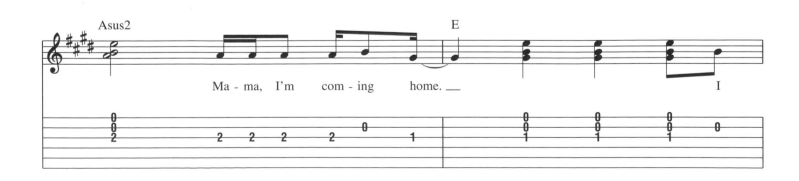

could be right, I could be wrong. It hurts so bad, it's been so long.

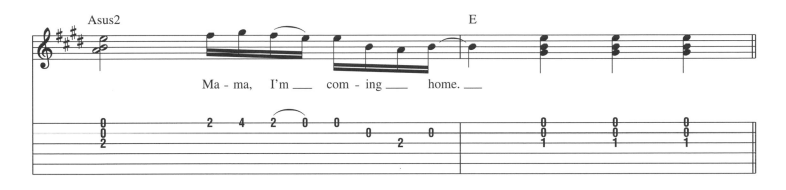

Ma - ma, I'm com - ing home.

Pre-Chorus

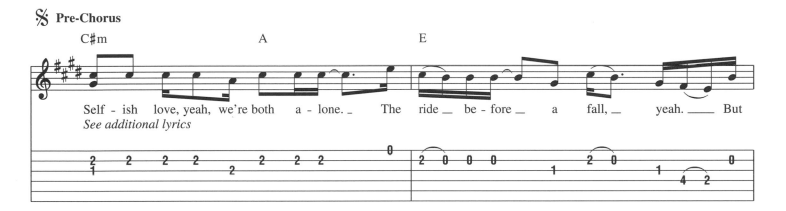

Self - ish love, yeah, we're both a - lone. The ride be - fore a fall, yeah. But
See additional lyrics

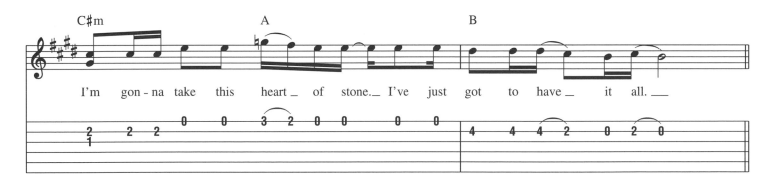

I'm gon - na take this heart of stone. I've just got to have it all.

Chorus

I've seen your face a {hun - dred / thou - sand} times

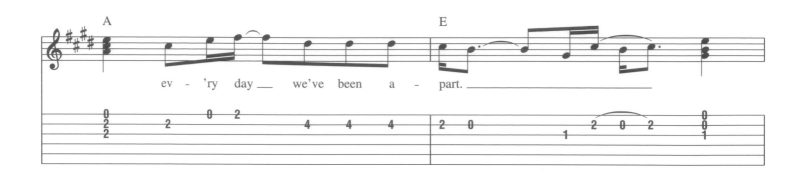

ev - 'ry day ___ we've been a - part._____

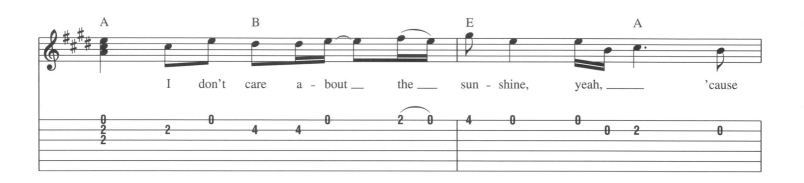

I don't care a - bout ___ the ___ sun - shine, yeah, _____ 'cause

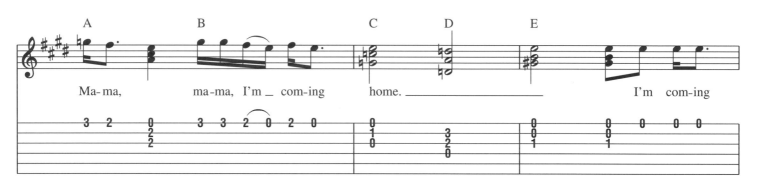

Ma - ma, ma - ma, I'm ___ com - ing home. _____ I'm com - ing

To Coda $\oplus$

Interlude

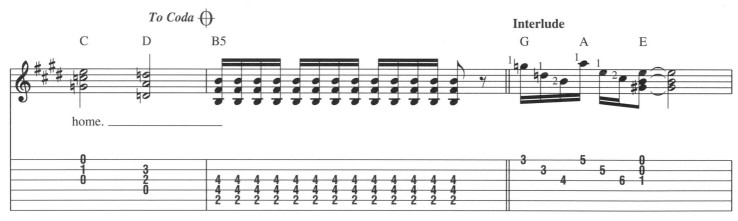

home. _____

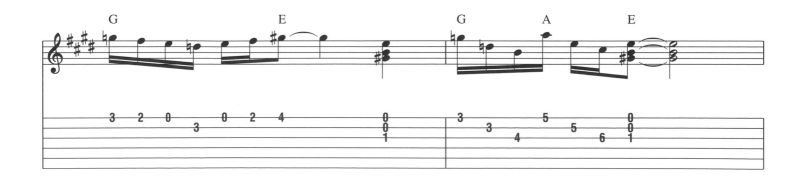

Additional Lyrics

Pre-Chorus You took me in and you drove me out,
Yeah, you had me hypnotized, yeah.
Lost and found and turned around
By the fire in your eyes.

Iron Man

Words and Music by Frank Iommi, John Osbourne, William Ward and Terence Butler

Strum Pattern: 2, 5

3. He was turned to steel in ___ the ___ great ___ mag - net - ic field,
4., 5. *See additional lyrics*

when he trav - elled time for ___ the ___ fu - ture of man - kind.

Bridge

No - bod - y wants ___ him, he just stares at the
See additional lyrics

world.

Plan - ning his venge - ance that he will soon un -

furl.

Interlude

Double-time feel

N.C. (C#m)

Play 4 times

End double-time feel

D.S. al Coda

B5

$\oplus$ **Coda**

Repeat and fade

B5   D5   E5   G5 F#5 G5 F#5 G5   D5   E5

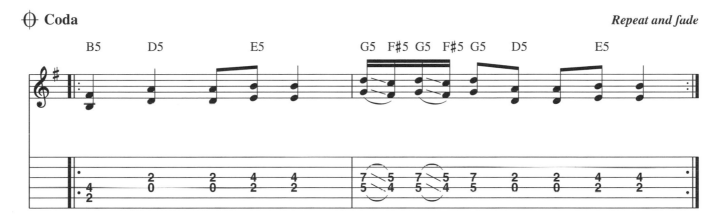

Additional Lyrics

2. Is he live or dead?
   I see thoughts within his head.
   We'll just pass him there.
   Why should we even care?

4. Now the time is here
   For Iron Man to spread fear.
   Vengeance from the grave,
   Kills the people he once saved.

Bridge Nobody wants him, they just turn their heads.
          Nobody helps him, now he has his revenge.

5. Heavy boots of lead
   Fills his victims full of dread,
   Running as fast as they can.
   Iron Man lives again!

No More Tears

Words and Music by Ozzy Osbourne, Zakk Wylde, Randy Castillo, Michael Inez and John Purdell

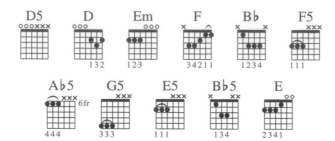

Strum Pattern: 5
Pick Pattern: 1

Drop D tuning:
(low to high) D–A–D–G–B–E

Intro
Moderate Rock

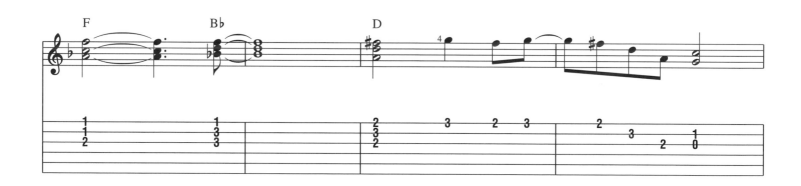

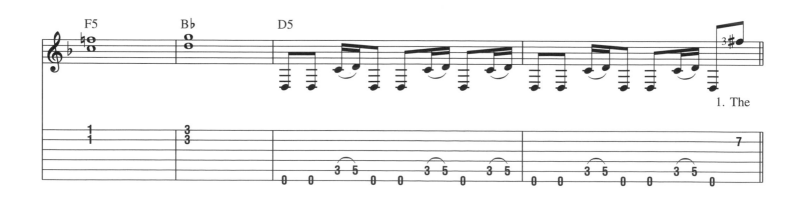

1. The

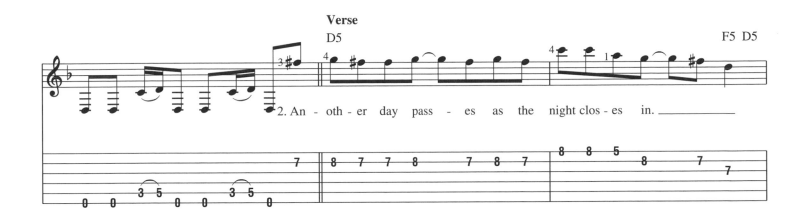

Verse

2. An - oth - er day pass - es as the night clos - es in. _____

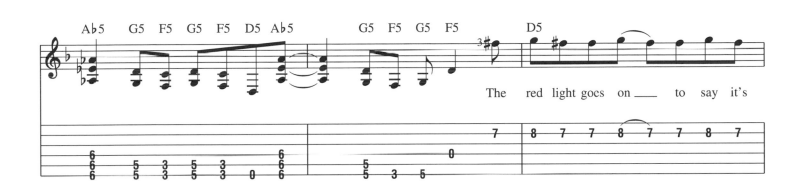

The red light goes on _____ to say it's

D.S. al Coda 1

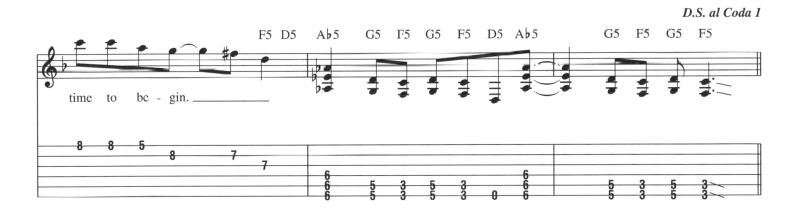

time to be - gin. _____

Coda 1

Chorus

1., 2.

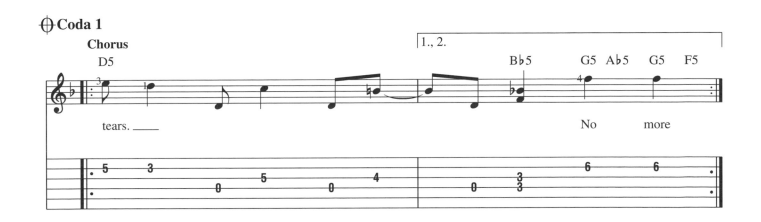

tears. _____   No   more

*w/ echo repeats

Additional Lyrics

Pre-Chorus 2. I see the man around the corner waiting, can he see me?
I close my eyes and wait to hear the sound of someone screaming here.

3. So now that it's over, can we just say goodbye?
I'd like to move on and make the most of the night.
Maybe a kiss before I leave you this way.
Your lips are so cold I don't know what else to say.

Pre-Chorus 3. I never wanted it to end this way, my love, my darling.
Believe me when I say to you in love I think I'm falling here.

Paranoid

Words and Music by Anthony Iommi, John Osbourne, William Ward and Terence Butler

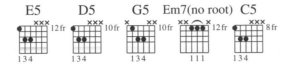

Strum Pattern: 1

Verse

2. All day long ___ I think ___ of things ___ but noth - ing seems ___ to
5. *See additional lyrics*

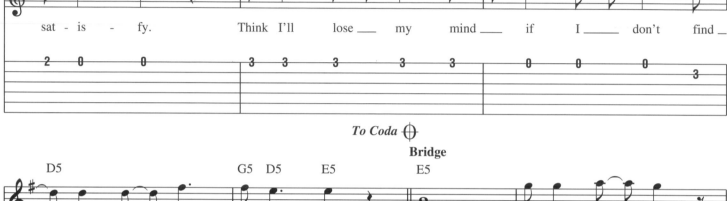

sat - is - fy. Think I'll lose ___ my mind ___ if I ___ don't find ___

To Coda ⊕

Bridge

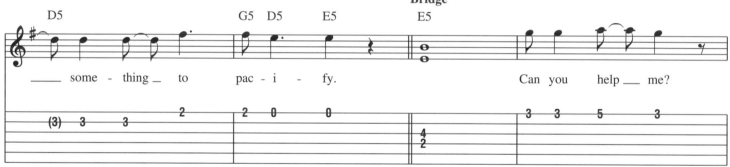

___ some - thing ___ to pac - i - fy. Can you help ___ me?

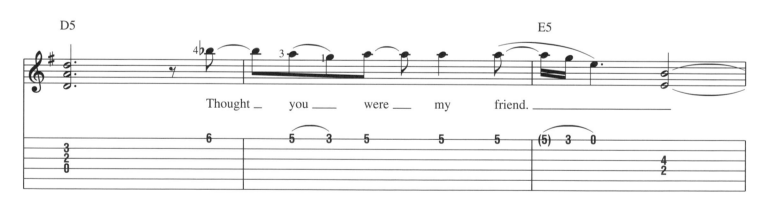

Thought ___ you ___ were ___ my friend. _____

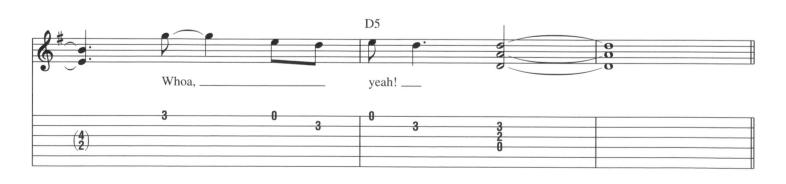

Whoa, _____ yeah! ___

Interlude

slight P.M. -

Verse

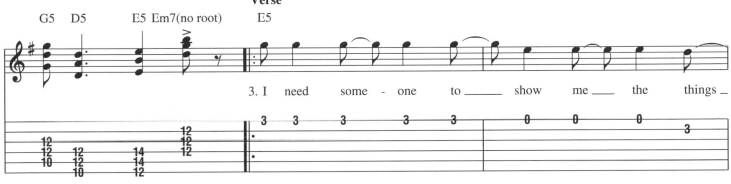

3. I need some-one to _____ show me _____ the things _____

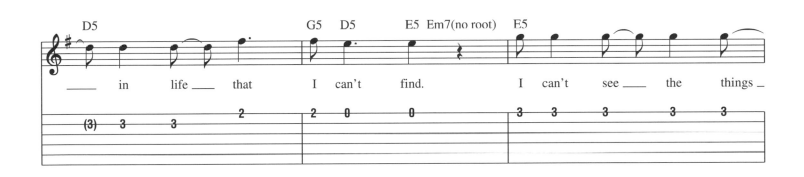

_____ in life _____ that I can't find. I can't see _____ the things _____

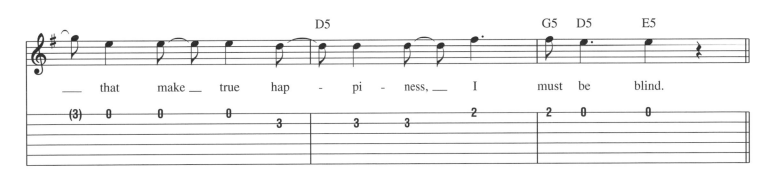

_____ that make _____ true hap - pi - ness, _____ I must be blind.

Guitar Solo

1 1/2

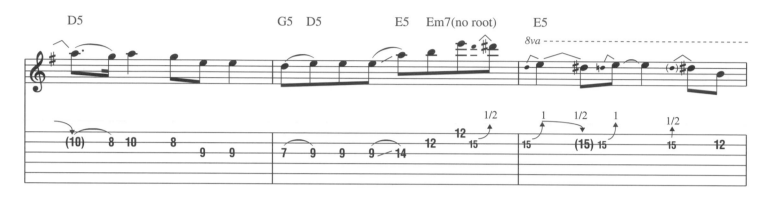

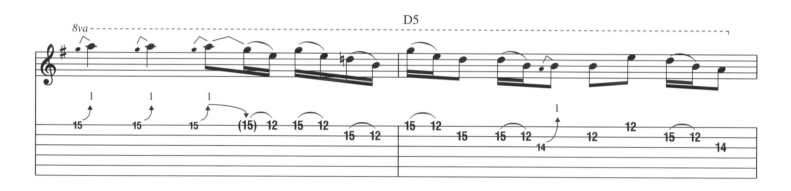

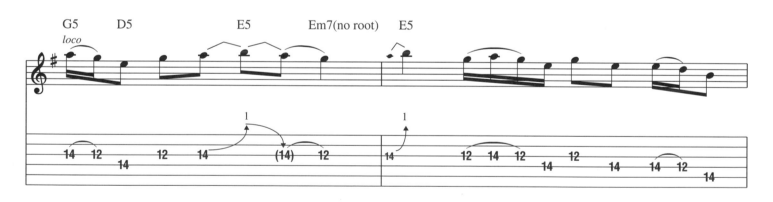

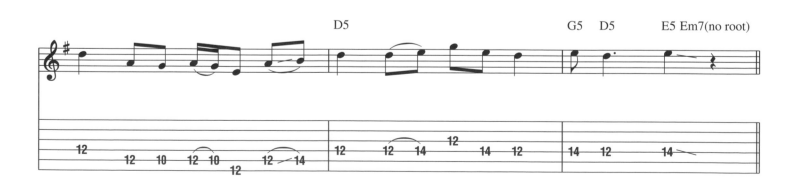

Interlude

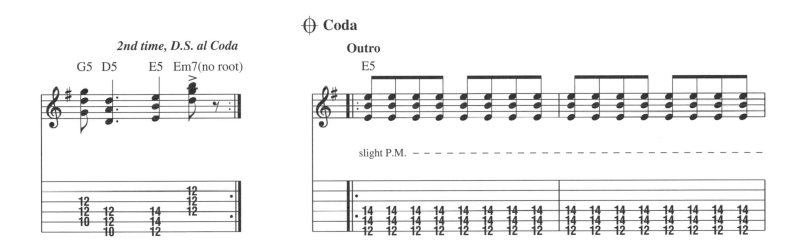

⊕ **Coda**

2nd time, D.S. al Coda

Outro

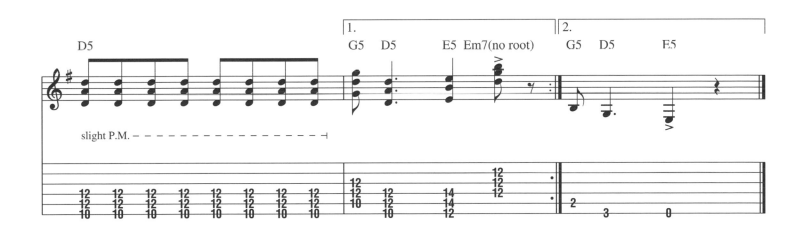

Additional Lyrics

4. Make a joke and I will sigh
   And you will laugh and I will cry.
   Happiness I cannot feel
   And love to me is so unreal.

5. And so as you hear these words
   Telling you now of my state.
   I tell you to enjoy life,
   I wish I could but it's too late.

Perry Mason

Words and Music by Ozzy Osbourne, Zakk Wylde and John Purdell

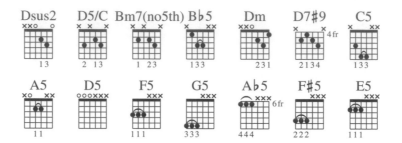

Drop D tuning:
(low to high) D–A–D–G–B–E

Intro

Moderately

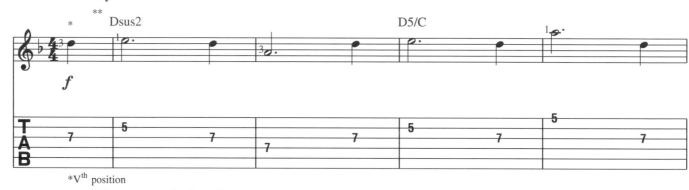

*Vᵗʰ position

**One strum per chord next 8 meas.

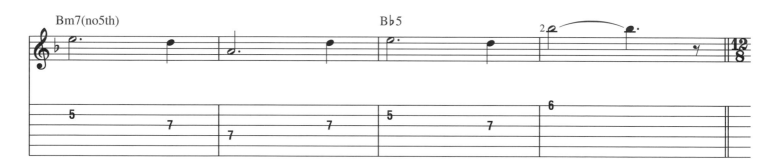

Strum Pattern: 8
Pick Pattern: 8

Guitar Solo

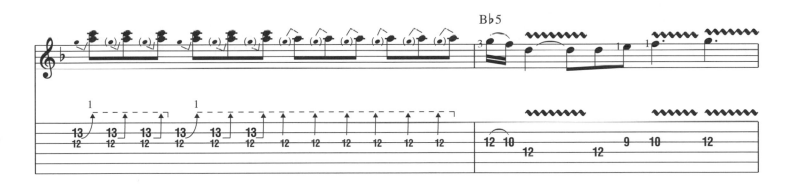

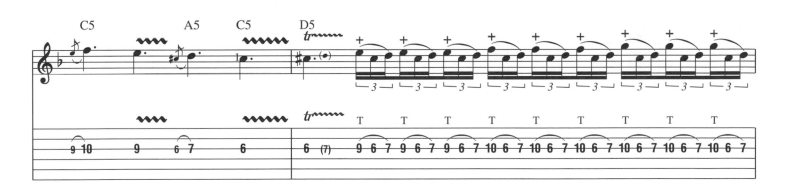

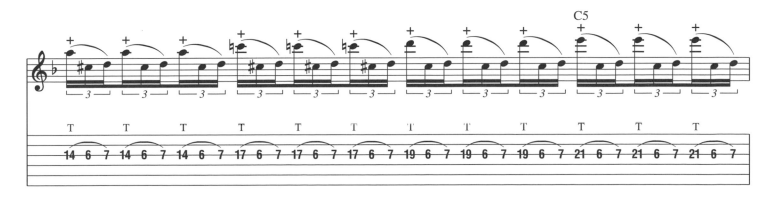

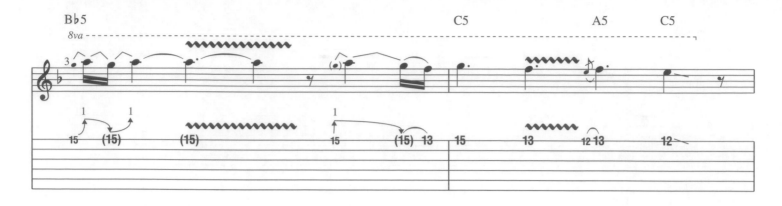

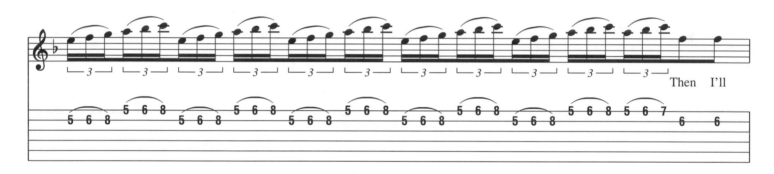

D.S. al Coda

Coda

Outro

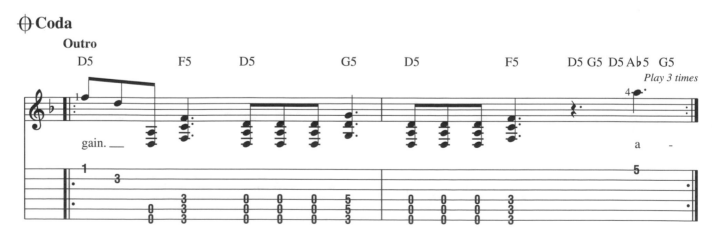

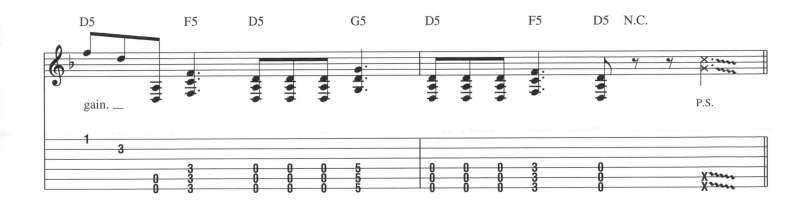

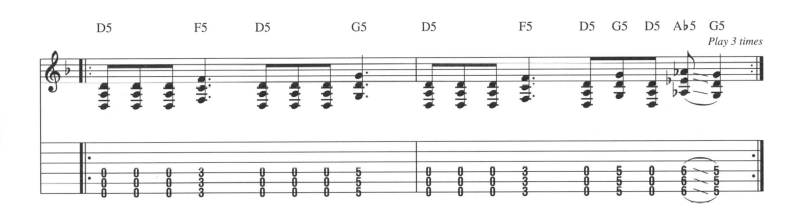

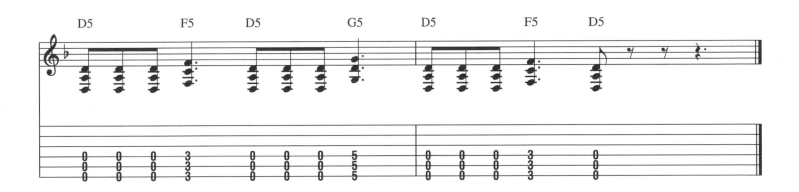

Additional Lyrics

2. Riding painted horses, oh, the kids they love it so.
   You can see it on their faces, how they live the wind to blow.
   Mind my own business, like my mama always said.
   But if I don't try to help'em, they could wind up on the front page.

Shot in the Dark

Words and Music by Ozzy Osbourne and Phil Soussan

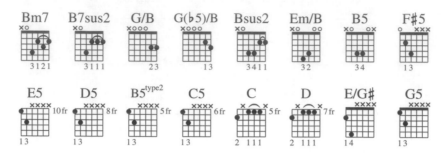

Tuning:
(low to high) F#–B–D–G–B–E

Strum Pattern: 6
Pick Pattern: 2, 6

Intro
Moderate Rock

*II nd position

*Bass plays E.

To Coda ⊕

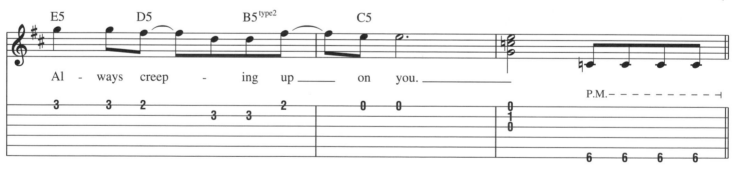

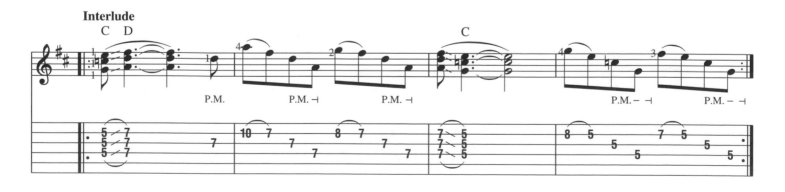

Guitar Solo

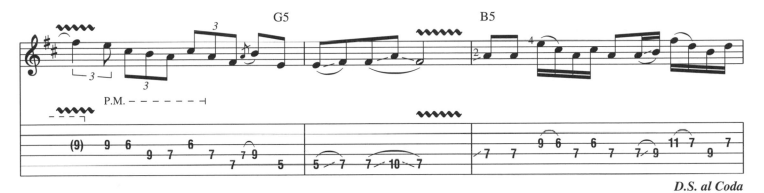

D.S. al Coda
(take 2nd ending)

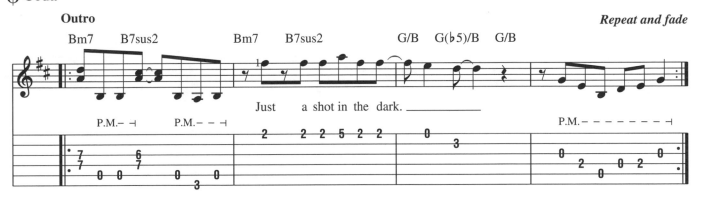

⊕ **Coda**

Outro   *Repeat and fade*

Just   a shot in the dark. _____

Additional Lyrics

2. Taught by the powers that preach over me.
I can hear their empty reason.
I wouldn't listen; I learned how to fight,
I opened up my mind to treason.

Pre-Chorus 2., 3. But just like the wounded and when it's too late.
They'll remember, they'll surrender.
Never a care for the people who hate,
Underestimate me now.

Chorus 2., 3. But a shot in the dark,
One step away from you.
Just a shot in the dark,
Nothing that you can do.
Just a shot in the dark.
Always creeping up on you.

Sweet Leaf

Words and Music by Frank Iommi, John Osbourne, William Ward and Terence Butler

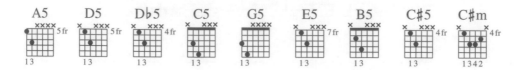

Strum Pattern: 2, 3
Pick Pattern: 1, 3

*Vth position

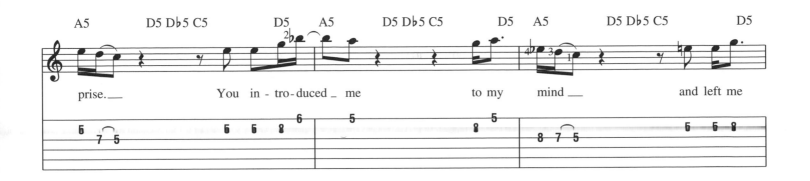

prise.___ You in-tro-duced _ me to my mind ___ and left me

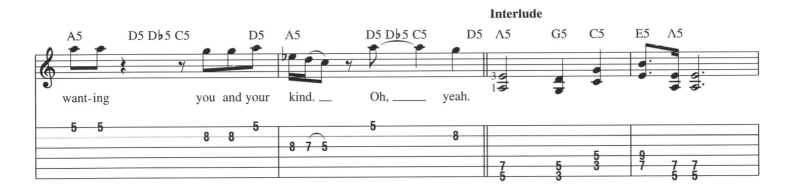

want-ing you and your kind. ___ Oh, ___ yeah.

Interlude

To Coda ⊕

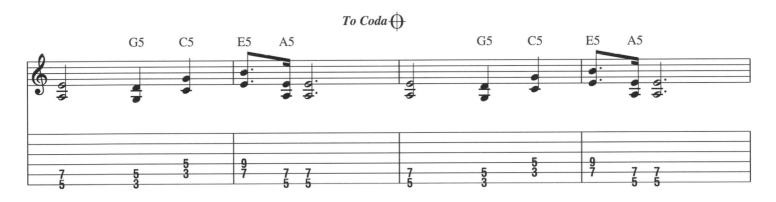

Bridge

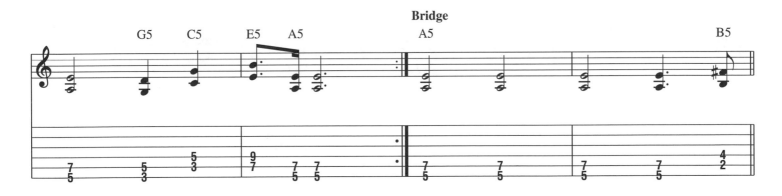

Faster

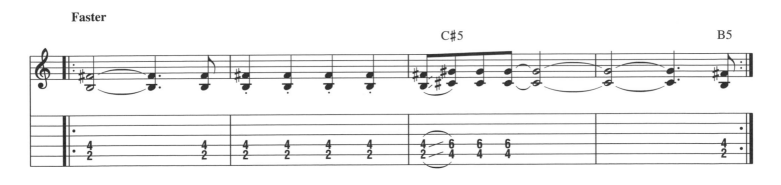

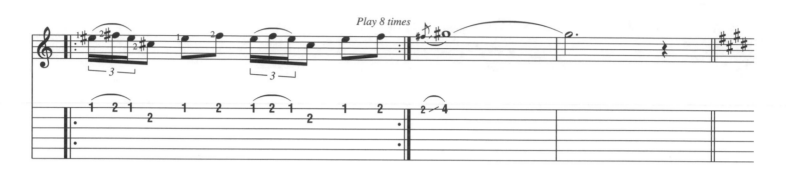

Guitar Solo

Interlude

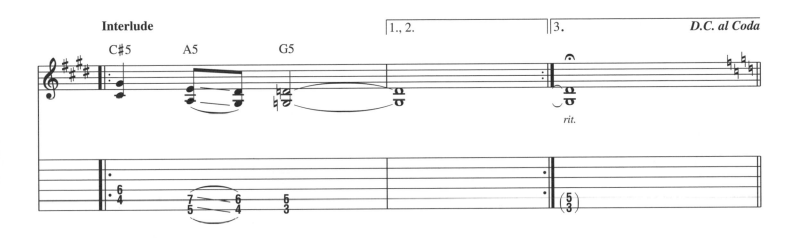

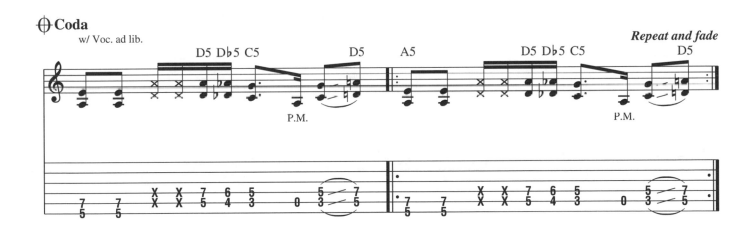

Additional Lyrics

2. My life was empty, forever on a down.
   Until you took me, showed me around.
   My life is free now, my life is clear.
   I love you sweet leaf, though you can't hear.

3. Straight people don't know what you're about.
   They put you down and shut you out.
   You gave to me a new belief.
   And soon the world will love you, sweet leaf.

War Pigs (Interpolating Luke's Wall)

Words and Music by Frank Iommi, John Osbourne, William Ward and Terence Butler

Intro
Moderately

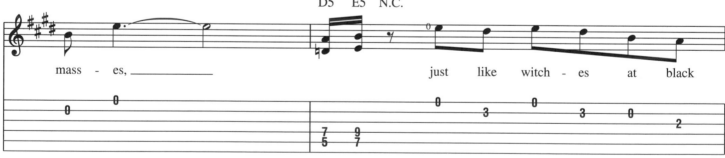

Verse

1. Gen - 'rals gath - ered in their mass - es,
2. *See additional lyrics*

just like witch - es at black mass - es. E - vil minds that plot de -

Strum Pattern: 2, 4
Pick Pattern: 2, 4

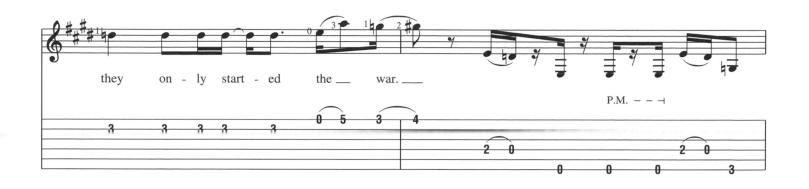

they on-ly start-ed the __ war. ___

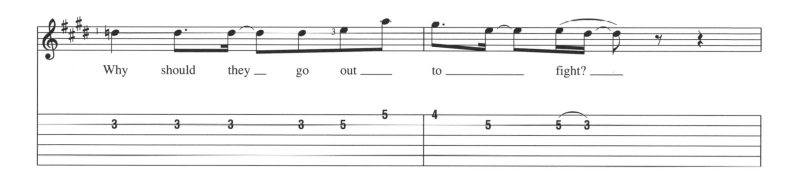

Why should they __ go out _____ to _____ fight? _____

Interlude
D5 E5 N.C. G5 F#5

They leave that _ all to the poor! ___ Yeah.

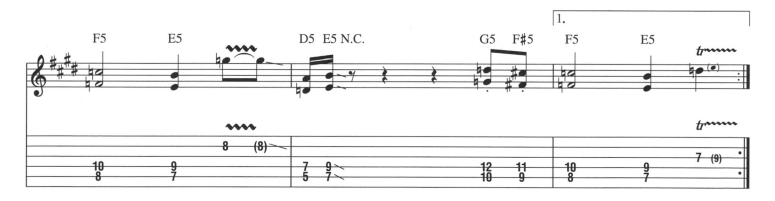

F5   E5   D5 E5 N.C.   G5 F#5   F5   E5

1.

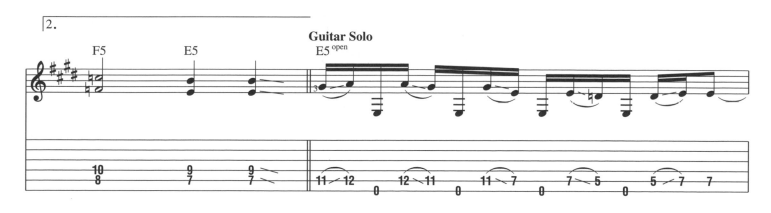

2.

Guitar Solo
E5 open

F5   E5

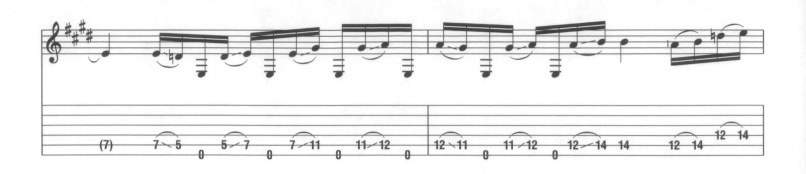

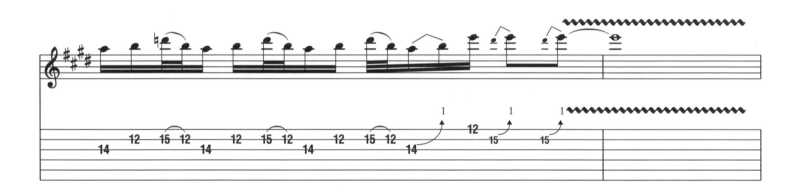

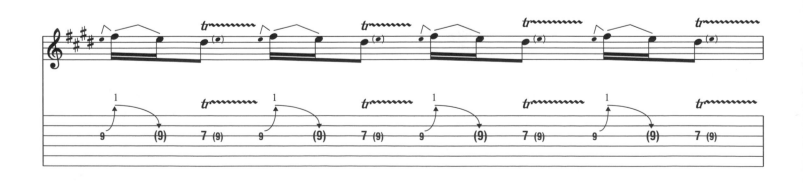

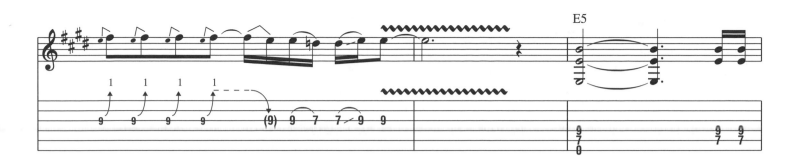

D.C. al Coda
(take repeat)

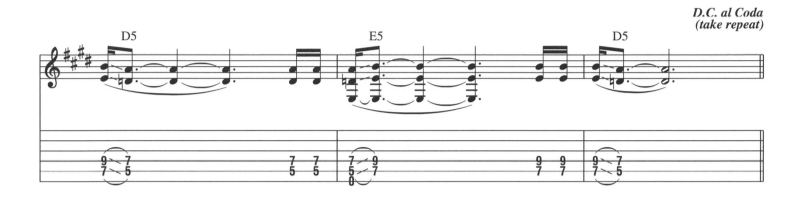

⊕ **Coda**

Interlude (Luke's Wall)

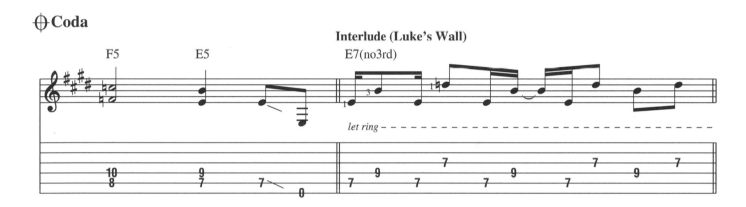

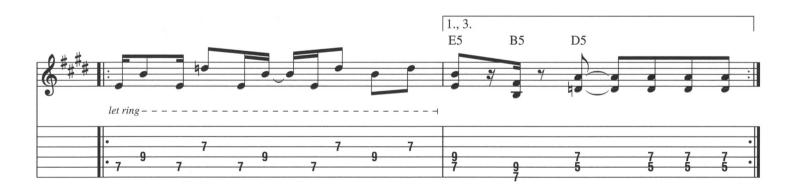

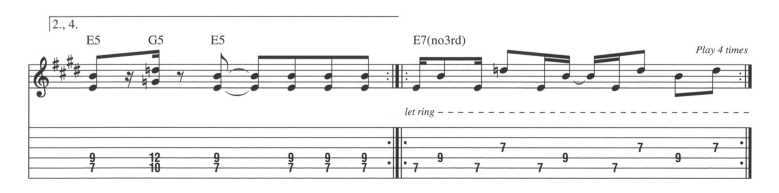

Additional Lyrics

2. Now in darkness, world stops turning,
Ashes where the bodies burning.
No more war pigs have the power.
Hand of God has struck the hour.
Day of judgment, God is calling,
On their knees, the war pigs crawling.
Begging mercies for their sins,
Satan laughing, spreads his wings.
Oh, Lord, yeah!

Bridge Time will tell on their power minds,
Making war just for fun.
Treating people just like pawns in chess,
Wait till their judgment day comes.
Yeah.